Perfect PENGUINS

EMPEROR PENGUIN

Written by Bethany Latham

Enslow PUBLISHING

Published in 2026 by Enslow Publishing, LLC
2544 Clinton Street
Buffalo, NY 14224

Written by: Bethany Latham
Edited by: Rebecca Phillips-Bartlett
Designed by: Amy Li

Cataloging-in-Publication Data

Names: Latham, Bethany, author.
Title: Emperor penguin / Bethany Latham.
Description: Buffalo, NY : Enslow Publishing, 2026. | Series: Perfect penguins | Includes glossary and index.
Identifiers: ISBN 9781978547377 (pbk.) | ISBN 9781978547384 (library bound) | ISBN 9781978547391 (ebook)
Subjects: LCSH: Emperor penguin--Juvenile literature.
Classification: LCC QL696.S473 L834 2026 | DDC 598.47--dc2

Manufactured in the United States of America

CPSIA compliance information: Batch #QW26ENS: For further information contact Enslow Publishing LLC, New York, New York at 1-800-398-2504.

Please visit our website, www.enslowpublishing.com. For a free color catalog of all our high-quality books, call toll free 1-800-398-2504 or fax 1-877-980-4454.

Find us on

IMAGE CREDITS

All images are courtesy of Shutterstock.com, unless otherwise stated.

Recurring – Martyshova Maria (doodles and arrows). Cover – Agami Photo Agency, Risto Raunio. 2–3 – vladsilver. 4–5 – robert mcgillivray, Maridav, fieldwork, polarman. 6–7 – Gonzalo Solari Cooke, GTW. 8–9 – Agami Photo Agency, Verbatim Vulgar Virtues 1, Danita Delimont. 10–11 – Foxberry, juan68. 12–13 – Mario_Hoppmann, polarman, Caroline Liekweg. 14–15 – Swaroop Pixs, Roger ARPS BPE1 CPAGB. 16–17 – Olga Geo, polarman. 18–19 – David Herraez Calzada, I. Noyan Yilmaz, SZakharov, Subphoto.com. 20–21 – Seemoregalery, Mozgova. 22–23 – Danita Delimont, vladsilver.

CONTENTS

WORDS THAT LOOK LIKE THIS CAN BE FOUND IN THE GLOSSARY ON PAGE 24.

EMPEROR PENGUINS

Penguins are a type of flightless bird. They live in many different places. Penguins are best known for their black and white feathers that look like jackets. There are 18 different species of penguin.

Emperor penguins are the biggest type of penguin. They can grow to around 4 feet (120 cm) tall. That is about the height of a tall six-year-old. Are you taller or smaller than an emperor penguin?

HABITAT

Emperor penguins only live in Antarctica. It gets very cold in Antarctica. Emperor penguins live on fast ice. Fast ice is made of big pieces of frozen ocean that are attached to the land.

An animal's natural home is called its habitat.

Some fast ice is so large that emperor penguins must travel 50 miles (80 km) to reach the ocean. Emperor penguins spend lots of time at sea. This is where they hunt to gain fat for the winter.

BODY

An emperor penguin's flippers and beak are quite small. This helps them avoid losing too much heat. Their feet contain fat to stop them freezing. They have strong claws to grip the ice.

Emperor penguins have two layers of feathers. The top layer of scale-like feathers is waterproof and windproof. When they clean themselves, emperor penguins cover their feathers with oil from their tails.

GETTING AROUND

Emperor penguins are amazing swimmers and divers. They are the deepest-diving penguin. They dive down to 1,640 feet (500 m) to catch fish. They can stay underwater for up to 22 minutes.

The color of an emperor penguin's feathers helps them camouflage themselves in the water.

Emperor penguins walk very slowly. To help them travel around more quickly on the ice, they toboggan. This is when penguins slide across the ice on their bellies and push with their feet.

LIFE CYCLE

A life cycle is the stages of an animal's life that lead to the animal having their own young.

Emperor penguins mate in March and April. To find a mate, penguins sing and bow to each other. Some penguins find their mate from the year before and have another egg together.

The mother lays one egg in May or June. The father cares for the egg while the mother fishes at sea. The father balances the egg on his feet to keep it warm.

The egg is kept in something called a brood pouch.

After around 70 days, the egg hatches. Emperor penguin chicks are gray and fluffy. Their feathers are not waterproof yet, so the chicks cannot get wet. Chicks gather in groups called crèches to stay safe.

As chicks grow up, they become juveniles. Juvenile emperor penguins are smaller than adults. They do not have any orange feathers yet. When emperor penguins reach five years old, they can have their own young.

Emperor penguins live for around 20 years in the wild.

FAMILY LIFE

Because it is very cold in the Antarctic, emperor penguins huddle together for warmth. One huddle can have up to 5,000 penguins. Penguins shuffle around to take turns on the outside where it is coldest.

AN EMPEROR PENGUIN COLONY

Emperor penguins live in large groups called colonies. Some colonies are so big they can be seen from space. There are over 50 emperor penguin colonies across the Antarctic.

DIET AND DANGERS

Emperor penguins mostly eat fish. They eat a lot of Antarctic silverfish, krill, and squid. Adult penguins eat 4.4 to 6.6 pounds (2 to 3 kg) per day. When building body fat, this amount can double.

ANTARCTIC KRILL

A diet is the type of food an animal eats.

Adult emperor penguins face danger in the ocean from creatures such as orcas and leopard seals. Emperor penguin chicks are also at risk of being eaten by birds called giant petrels.

LEOPARD SEAL

ORCA

PROTECT THE PENGUINS

Emperor penguins are near threatened. This means the number of penguins is falling. Climate change is melting the ice, and humans are fishing too much. This means the penguins cannot catch as many fish.

Some people are helping emperor penguins by making safe areas in the ocean called marine protected areas. People cannot fish in these areas. This makes sure the penguins have enough fish to eat.

You can adopt a penguin with some animal charities.

PERFECT PENGUINS

Emperor penguins are amazing birds. We have seen how they are experts at living in a cold habitat. What are some ways you adapt to your surroundings when it gets cold?

Emperor penguins are great at looking after each other. How do you look after your friends and family?

What was your favorite emperor penguin fact? Do you think you would like to meet an emperor penguin?

GLOSSARY

ADOPT	giving money to a charity to help look after animals
CAMOUFLAGE	to hide by blending into the surroundings
CLIMATE CHANGE	a change in the typical weather or temperature of a large area
MARINE	things relating to the ocean
MATE	to produce young with an animal of the same species
SPECIES	a group of very similar animals or plants that can create young together

INDEX